· Grandma's ·
OLD-FASHIONED
· Cookies

Publications International, Ltd.

Contents

Favorites

CHOCOLATE–DIPPED ALMOND HORNS

1½ cups powdered sugar
1 cup butter or margarine, softened
2 egg yolks
1½ teaspoons vanilla
2 cups all-purpose flour
½ cup ground almonds
1 teaspoon cream of tartar
1 teaspoon baking soda
1 cup semisweet chocolate chips, melted
Powdered sugar

Preheat oven to 325°F. In large bowl, combine powdered sugar and butter. Beat at medium speed until creamy. Add egg yolks and vanilla; continue beating until well blended. Reduce speed to low. Add flour, almonds, cream of tartar and baking soda. Continue beating until well mixed. Shape into 1-inch balls. Roll balls into 2-inch ropes; shape into crescents. Place 2 inches apart on cookie sheets. Flatten slightly with bottom of glass covered in waxed paper. Bake for 8 to 10 minutes or until set. (Cookies do not brown.) Cool completely. Dip half of each cookie into chocolate; sprinkle remaining half with powdered sugar. Refrigerate until set.

Makes about 3 dozen cookies

OATMEAL APPLE COOKIES

¾ **CRISCO® Stick or ¾ cup CRISCO®**
   All-Vegetable Shortening
1¼ **cups firmly packed brown sugar**
 1 **egg**
¼ **cup milk**
1½ **teaspoons vanilla**
 1 **cup all-purpose flour**
1¼ **teaspoons ground cinnamon**
½ **teaspoon salt**
¼ **teaspoon baking soda**
¼ **teaspoon ground nutmeg**
 3 **cups quick oats (not instant or**
   old-fashioned)
 1 **cup peeled, diced apples**
¾ **cup raisins (optional)**
¾ **cup coarsely chopped walnuts (optional)**

1. Preheat oven to 375°F. Grease cookie sheet with shortening.

2. Combine shortening, sugar, egg, milk and vanilla in large bowl. Beat at medium speed of electric mixer until well blended.

3. Combine flour, cinnamon, salt, baking soda and nutmeg in small bowl. Mix into creamed mixture at low speed until just blended. Stir in, one at a time, oats, apples, raisins and nuts with spoon.

4. Drop rounded tablespoonfuls of dough 2 inches apart onto cookie sheet.

5. Bake at 375°F for 13 minutes or until set. Cool 2 minutes on cookie sheet. Remove to wire rack. Cool completely. *Makes about 2½ dozen cookies*

PEANUT BUTTER SENSATIONS

½ **CRISCO® Stick or ½ cup CRISCO®**
   All-Vegetable Shortening
 1 **cup JIF® Creamy Peanut Butter**
¾ **cup granulated sugar**
½ **cup firmly packed brown sugar**
 1 **tablespoon milk**
 1 **teaspoon vanilla**
 1 **egg**
1¼ **cups all-purpose flour**
¾ **teaspoon baking soda**
½ **teaspoon baking powder**
¼ **teaspoon salt**

1. Preheat oven to 375°F.

2. Combine shortening, peanut butter, granulated sugar, brown sugar, milk and vanilla in large bowl. Beat at medium speed of electric mixer until well blended. Beat in egg.

3. Combine flour, baking soda, baking powder and salt in small bowl. Mix into creamed mixture at low speed until just blended. Drop rounded tablespoonfuls of dough 2 inches apart onto ungreased cookie sheet. Make crisscross pattern on dough with floured fork.

4. Bake at 375°F for 8 to 10 minutes. Cool 2 minutes on cookie sheet. Remove to wire rack. Cool completely. *Makes about 2 dozen cookies*

Oatmeal Apple Cookies

COCOA SNICKERDOODLES

1 cup butter or margarine, softened
¾ cup firmly packed brown sugar
¾ cup plus 2 tablespoons granulated sugar, divided
2 eggs
2 cups uncooked rolled oats
1½ cups all-purpose flour
¼ cup plus 2 tablespoons unsweetened cocoa powder, divided
1 teaspoon baking soda
2 tablespoons ground cinnamon

Preheat oven to 375°F. Lightly grease cookie sheets or line with parchment paper. Beat butter, brown sugar and ¾ cup granulated sugar in large bowl until light and fluffy. Add eggs; mix well. Combine oats, flour, ¼ cup cocoa and baking soda in medium bowl. Stir into butter mixture until blended. Mix remaining 2 tablespoons granulated sugar, cinnamon and remaining 2 tablespoons cocoa in small bowl. Drop dough by rounded teaspoonfuls into cinnamon mixture; toss to coat. Place 2 inches apart on prepared cookie sheets. Bake 8 to 10 minutes or until firm in center. *Do not overbake.* Remove to wire racks to cool.

Makes about 4½ dozen cookies

SPICY PUMPKIN COOKIES

2 CRISCO® Sticks or 2 cups CRISCO® All-Vegetable Shortening
2 cups sugar
1 can (16 ounces) solid pack pumpkin
2 eggs
2 teaspoons vanilla
4 cups all-purpose flour
2 teaspoons baking powder
2 teaspoons ground cinnamon
1 teaspoon salt
1 teaspoon baking soda
1 teaspoon ground nutmeg
½ teaspoon ground allspice
2 cups raisins
1 cup chopped nuts

1. Preheat oven to 350°F.

2. Combine shortening, sugar, pumpkin, eggs and vanilla in large bowl; beat well.

3. Combine flour, baking powder, cinnamon, salt, baking soda, nutmeg and allspice in medium bowl. Add to pumpkin mixture; mix well. Stir in raisins and nuts. Drop rounded teaspoonfuls of dough, 2 inches apart, onto greased cookie sheet.

4. Bake at 350°F for 12 to 15 minutes. Cool on wire rack. If desired, frost with vanilla frosting.

Makes about 7 dozen cookies

Chocolate–Peanut Cookies (page 20),
Cocoa Snickerdoodles

RASPBERRY ALMOND SANDWICH COOKIES

1 package DUNCAN HINES® Golden Sugar Cookie Mix
1 egg
¼ cup CRISCO® Oil
1 tablespoon water
¾ teaspoon almond extract
1⅓ cups sliced natural almonds, broken
Seedless red raspberry jam

1. Preheat oven to 375°F.

2. Combine cookie mix, egg, oil, water and almond extract in large bowl. Stir until thoroughly blended. Drop half the dough by level measuring teaspoons 2 inches apart onto ungreased cookie sheets. (It is a small amount of dough but will spread during baking to 1½ to 1¾ inches.)

3. Place almonds on waxed paper. Drop other half of dough by level measuring teaspoons onto nuts. Place almond side up 2 inches apart on cookie sheets.

4. Bake both plain and almond cookies at 375°F for 6 minutes or until set but not browned. Cool 1 minute on cookie sheets. Remove to wire racks. Cool completely.

5. Spread bottoms of plain cookies with jam; top with almond cookies. Press together to make sandwiches. Store in airtight containers.

Makes 6 dozen sandwich cookies

OLD–FASHIONED OATMEAL COOKIES

¾ CRISCO® Stick or ¾ cup CRISCO® All-Vegetable Shortening
1¼ cups firmly packed brown sugar
1 egg
⅓ cup milk
1½ teaspoons vanilla
1 cup all-purpose flour
½ teaspoon baking soda
½ teaspoon salt
¼ teaspoon ground cinnamon
3 cups quick oats (not instant or old-fashioned)
1 cup raisins
1 cup coarsely chopped walnuts

1. Preheat oven to 375°F. Grease cookie sheet.

2. Combine shortening, sugar, egg, milk and vanilla in large bowl. Beat at medium speed of electric mixer until well blended.

3. Combine flour, baking soda, salt and cinnamon in small bowl. Mix into creamed mixture at low speed until just blended. Stir in oats, raisins and nuts with spoon.

4. Drop rounded tablespoonfuls of dough 2 inches apart onto cookie sheet.

5. Bake at 375°F for 10 to 12 minutes or until lightly browned. Cool 2 minutes on cookie sheet. Remove to wire rack. Cool completely.

Makes about 2½ dozen cookies

Raspberry Almond Sandwich Cookies

ULTIMATE SUGAR COOKIES

1¼ cups granulated sugar
1 CRISCO® Stick or 1 cup CRISCO®
   All-Vegetable Shortening
2 eggs
¼ cup light corn syrup or regular pancake
   syrup
1 tablespoon vanilla
3 cups all-purpose flour (plus
   4 tablespoons), divided
¾ teaspoon baking powder
½ teaspoon baking soda
½ teaspoon salt
   Granulated sugar or colored sugar
   crystals

1. Place sugar and shortening in large bowl. Beat at medium speed of electric mixer until well blended. Add eggs, syrup and vanilla; beat until well blended and fluffy.

2. Combine 3 cups flour, baking powder, baking soda and salt in medium bowl. Add gradually to shortening mixture, beating at low speed until well blended.

3. Divide dough into 4 equal pieces; shape each piece into disk. Wrap with plastic wrap. Refrigerate 1 hour or until firm.

4. Preheat oven to 375°F. Place sheets of foil on countertop for cooling cookies.

5. Sprinkle about 1 tablespoon flour on large sheet of waxed paper. Place disk of dough on floured paper; flatten slightly with hands. Turn dough over; cover with another large sheet of waxed paper. Roll dough to ¼-inch thickness. Remove top sheet of waxed paper. Cut into desired shapes with floured cookie cutters. Place 2 inches apart on ungreased cookie sheet. Repeat with remaining dough.

6. Sprinkle with granulated sugar.

7. Bake one cookie sheet at a time at 375°F for 5 to 7 minutes or until edges of cookies are lightly browned. *Do not overbake.* Cool 2 minutes on cookie sheet. Remove cookies to foil to cool completely.   *Makes about 3½ dozen cookies*

Ultimate Sugar Cookies

KENTUCKY BOURBON PECAN TARTS

Cream Cheese Pastry (recipe follows)
2 eggs
½ cup granulated sugar
½ cup KARO® Light or Dark Corn Syrup
2 tablespoons bourbon
1 tablespoon MAZOLA® Margarine, melted
½ teaspoon vanilla
1 cup chopped pecans
Powdered sugar (optional)

Preheat oven to 350°F. Prepare Cream Cheese Pastry. Divide dough in half; set aside one half. On floured surface, roll out pastry to ⅛-inch thickness. *If necessary, add small amount of flour to keep pastry from sticking.* Cut into 12 (2¼-inch) rounds. Press evenly into bottoms and up sides of 1¾-inch muffin pan cups. Repeat with remaining pastry. Refrigerate.

In medium bowl, beat eggs slightly. Stir in granulated sugar, corn syrup, bourbon, margarine and vanilla until well blended. Spoon 1 heaping teaspoon pecans into each pastry-lined cup; top with 1 tablespoon corn syrup mixture.

Bake 20 to 25 minutes or until lightly browned and toothpick inserted into center comes out clean. Cool in pans 5 minutes. Remove; cool completely on wire rack. If desired, sprinkle cookies with powdered sugar.

Makes about 2 dozen cookies

CREAM CHEESE PASTRY

1 cup all-purpose flour
¾ teaspoon baking powder
Pinch salt
½ cup MAZOLA® Margarine, softened
1 package (3 ounces) cream cheese, softened
2 teaspoons sugar

In small bowl, combine flour, baking powder and salt. In large bowl, mix margarine, cream cheese and sugar until well combined. Stir in flour mixture until well blended. Press firmly into ball with hands.

Prep Time: 45 minutes
Bake Time: 25 minutes, plus cooling

Top to bottom: Brandy Lace Cookies (page 16), Kentucky Bourbon Pecan Tarts

AUSTRIAN TEA COOKIES

1½ cups sugar, divided
½ cup butter, softened
½ cup vegetable shortening
1 egg, beaten
½ teaspoon vanilla extract
2 cups all-purpose flour
2 cups ALMOND DELIGHT® Brand Cereal, crushed to 1 cup
½ teaspoon baking powder
¼ teaspoon ground cinnamon
14 ounces almond paste
2 egg whites
5 tablespoons raspberry or apricot jam, warmed

In large bowl, beat 1 cup sugar, butter and shortening. Add egg and vanilla; mix well. Stir in flour, cereal, baking powder and cinnamon until well blended. Refrigerate 1 to 2 hours or until firm.

Preheat oven to 350°F. Roll dough out on lightly floured surface to ¼-inch thickness; cut into 2-inch circles with floured cookie cutter. Place on ungreased cookie sheet; set aside. In small bowl, beat almond paste, egg whites and remaining ½ cup sugar until smooth. With pastry tube fitted with medium-sized star tip, pipe almond paste mixture ½ inch thick on top of each cookie along outside edge. Place ¼ teaspoon jam in center of each cookie, spreading out to paste. Bake 8 to 10 minutes or until lightly browned. Let stand 1 minute before removing from cookie sheet. Cool on wire rack. *Makes about 3½ dozen cookies*

BRANDY LACE COOKIES

¼ cup sugar
¼ cup MAZOLA® Margarine
¼ cup KARO® Light or Dark Corn Syrup
½ cup all-purpose flour
¼ cup very finely chopped pecans or walnuts
2 tablespoons brandy
Melted white and/or semisweet chocolate (optional)

Preheat oven to 350°F. Lightly grease and flour cookie sheets.

In small saucepan, combine sugar, margarine and corn syrup. Bring to boil over medium heat, stirring constantly. Remove from heat. Stir in flour, pecans and brandy. Drop 12 evenly spaced half teaspoonfuls of batter onto prepared cookie sheets.

Bake 6 minutes or until golden. Cool 1 to 2 minutes or until cookies can be lifted but are still warm and pliable; remove with spatula. Curl around handle of wooden spoon; slide off when crisp. If cookies harden before curling, return to oven to soften. If desired, drizzle with melted chocolate. *Makes 4 to 5 dozen cookies*

Prep Time: 30 minutes
Bake Time: 6 minutes, plus curling and cooling

Austrian Tea Cookies

PEANUT BUTTER CHOCOLATE CHIPPERS

**1 cup creamy or chunky peanut butter
1 cup firmly packed light brown sugar
1 large egg
¾ cup milk chocolate chips
Granulated sugar**

1. Preheat oven to 350°F.

2. Combine peanut butter, brown sugar and egg in medium bowl with mixing spoon until well blended. Add chips; mix well.

3. Roll heaping tablespoonfuls of dough into 1½-inch balls. Place balls 2 inches apart on *ungreased* cookie sheets.

4. Dip table fork into granulated sugar; press criss-cross fashion onto each ball, flattening to ½-inch thickness.

5. Bake 12 minutes or until set. Let cookies stand on cookie sheets 2 minutes. Remove cookies with spatula to wire racks; cool completely. Store tightly covered at room temperature or freeze up to 3 months.   *Makes about 2 dozen cookies*

CHOCOLATE CHIP SANDWICH COOKIES

COOKIES

    1 package DUNCAN HINES® Chocolate Chip
       Cookie Mix
    1 egg
    ⅓ cup CRISCO® Oil
    3 tablespoons water

CREAM FILLING

    1½ cups marshmallow creme
    ¾ cup butter or margarine, softened
    2½ cups powdered sugar
    1½ teaspoons vanilla extract

1. Preheat oven to 375°F.

2. For Cookies, combine cookie mix, egg, oil and water in large bowl. Stir until thoroughly blended. Drop by rounded teaspoonfuls 2 inches apart onto ungreased cookie sheets. Bake at 375°F for 8 to 10 minutes or until light golden brown. Cool 1 minute on cookie sheets. Remove to wire racks.

3. For Cream Filling, combine marshmallow creme and butter in large bowl. Add powdered sugar and vanilla extract, beating until smooth.

4. To assemble, spread bottoms of half the cookies with 1 tablespoon cream filling; top with remaining cookies. Press together to make sandwich cookies. Refrigerate to quickly firm the filling, if desired.

Makes about 24 sandwich cookies

TIP: After chilling the assembled cookies, wrap individually in plastic wrap. Store in the refrigerator until ready to serve.

CHOCOLATE–PEANUT COOKIES

    1 cup butter or margarine, softened
    ¾ cup granulated sugar
    ¾ cup firmly packed light brown sugar
    2 eggs
    1 teaspoon vanilla
    1 teaspoon baking soda
    ¼ teaspoon salt
    2¼ cups all-purpose flour
    2 cups chocolate-covered peanuts

Preheat oven to 375°F. Line cookie sheets with parchment paper or leave ungreased. Beat butter, granulated sugar, brown sugar, eggs and vanilla in large bowl with electric mixer until fluffy. Beat in baking soda and salt. Stir in flour to make stiff dough. Blend in chocolate-covered peanuts. Drop by rounded teaspoonfuls 2 inches apart onto cookie sheets. Bake 9 to 11 minutes or until just barely golden. *Do not overbake.* Remove to wire racks to cool.   *Makes about 5 dozen cookies*

Chocolate Chip Sandwich Cookies

ORIGINAL NESTLÉ® TOLL HOUSE® CHOCOLATE CHIP COOKIES

2¼ cups all-purpose flour
1 teaspoon baking soda
1 teaspoon salt
1 cup (2 sticks) butter, softened
¾ cup granulated sugar
¾ cup firmly packed brown sugar
1 teaspoon vanilla extract
2 eggs
2 cups (12-ounce package) NESTLÉ®
   TOLL HOUSE® Semi-Sweet Chocolate
   Morsels
1 cup chopped nuts

COMBINE flour, baking soda and salt in small bowl. Beat butter, granulated sugar, brown sugar and vanilla in large mixing bowl. Add eggs one at a time, beating well after each addition; gradually beat in flour mixture. Stir in morsels and nuts. Drop by rounded tablespoons onto ungreased cookie sheets.

BAKE in preheated 375°F oven for 9 to 11 minutes or until golden brown. Let stand for 2 minutes; remove to wire racks to cool completely.

Makes about 5 dozen cookies

COWBOY COOKIES

½ cup butter or margarine, softened
½ cup firmly packed light brown sugar
¼ cup granulated sugar
1 egg
1 teaspoon vanilla
1 cup all-purpose flour
2 tablespoons unsweetened cocoa
½ teaspoon baking powder
¼ teaspoon baking soda
1 cup uncooked rolled oats
1 cup (6 ounces) semisweet chocolate
   chips
½ cup raisins
½ cup chopped nuts

Preheat oven to 375°F. Lightly grease cookie sheets or line with parchment paper. Beat butter, brown sugar and granulated sugar in large bowl with electric mixer until blended. Add egg and vanilla; beat until fluffy. Combine flour, cocoa, baking powder and baking soda in small bowl; stir into creamed mixture with oats, chocolate chips, raisins and nuts. Drop dough by teaspoonfuls 2 inches apart onto prepared cookie sheets. Bake 10 to 12 minutes or until lightly browned around edges. Remove to wire racks to cool.

Makes about 4 dozen cookies

Original Nestlé® Toll House® Chocolate Chip Cookies

ULTIMATE CHOCOLATE CHIP COOKIES

¾ **CRISCO® Stick or ¾ cup CRISCO®**
   All-Vegetable Shortening
1¼ **cups firmly packed brown sugar**
 2 **tablespoons milk**
 1 **tablespoon vanilla**
 1 **egg**
1¾ **cups all-purpose flour**
 1 **teaspoon salt**
 ¾ **teaspoon baking soda**
 1 **cup semi-sweet chocolate chips**
 1 **cup coarsely chopped pecans***

*You may substitute an additional ½ cup semi-sweet chocolate chips for the pecans.

1. Preheat oven to 375°F.

2. Combine shortening, sugar, milk and vanilla in large bowl. Beat at medium speed of electric mixer until well blended. Beat in egg.

3. Combine flour, salt and baking soda in small bowl. Mix into creamed mixture at low speed until just blended. Stir in chocolate chips and nuts.

4. Drop rounded tablespoonfuls of dough 3 inches apart onto ungreased cookie sheet.

5. Bake at 375°F for 8 to 10 minutes for chewy cookies (they will look light and moist—*do not overbake*), 11 to 13 minutes for crisp cookies. Cool 2 minutes on cookie sheet. Remove to wire rack. Cool completely.   *Makes about 3 dozen cookies*

Variations for Ultimate Chocolate Chip Cookies

DRIZZLE: Combine 1 teaspoon CRISCO® All-Vegetable Shortening and 1 cup semi-sweet chocolate chips or 1 cup white melting chocolate, cut into small pieces, in microwave-safe measuring cup. Microwave at 50% (MEDIUM). Stir after 1 minute. Repeat until smooth (or melt on rangetop in small saucepan on very low heat). To thin, add a little more shortening. Drizzle back and forth over cookie. Sprinkle with nuts before chocolate hardens, if desired. To quickly harden chocolate, place cookies in refrigerator for a few minutes.

CHOCOLATE DIPPED: Melt chocolate as directed for Drizzle. Dip one end of cooled cookie halfway up in chocolate. Sprinkle with finely chopped nuts before chocolate hardens. Place on waxed paper until chocolate is firm. To quickly harden chocolate, place cookies in refrigerator for a few minutes.

Clockwise from top: Old-Fashioned Oatmeal Cookies (page 10),
Peanut Butter Sensations (page 6),
Ultimate Chocolate Chip Cookies

Bar Cookies

CHOCOLATE CHIP SHORTBREAD

½ **cup butter, softened**
½ **cup sugar**
 1 **teaspoon vanilla**
 1 **cup all-purpose flour**
¼ **teaspoon salt**
½ **cup mini semisweet chocolate chips**

Preheat oven to 375°F. Beat butter and sugar in large bowl with electric mixer at medium speed until light and fluffy. Beat in vanilla. Add flour and salt. Stir in chips.

Divide dough in half. Press each half into ungreased 8-inch round cake pan. Bake 12 minutes or until edges are golden brown. Score shortbread with sharp knife, taking care not to cut completely through shortbread. Make 8 wedges per pan.

Let pans stand on wire racks 10 minutes. Invert shortbread onto wire racks; cool completely. Break into wedges.   *Makes 16 cookies*

CALIFORNIA APRICOT POWER BARS

2 cups California dried apricot halves, coarsely chopped (12 ounces)
2½ cups pecans, coarsely chopped (10 ounces)
1¼ cups pitted dates, coarsely chopped (8 ounces)
1¼ cups whole wheat flour
1 teaspoon baking powder
1 cup firmly packed brown sugar
3 large eggs
¼ cup apple juice or water
1½ teaspoons vanilla

Preheat oven to 350°F. Line 15½×10½×1-inch jelly-roll pan with foil. In large bowl, stir together apricots, pecans and dates; divide in half. In small bowl, combine flour and baking powder; add to half of fruit-nut mixture. Toss to coat. In medium bowl, combine brown sugar, eggs, apple juice and vanilla; stir into flour mixture until thoroughly moistened. Spread batter evenly into prepared pan. Lightly press remaining fruit-nut mixture on top.

Bake 20 minutes or until bars are golden and spring back when pressed lightly. Cool in pan 5 minutes. Turn out onto wire rack; cool 45 minutes. Peel off foil and cut into bars. Store in airtight container. Bars may be frozen.

Makes about 32 bars

Favorite recipe from California Apricot Advisory Board

"CORDIALLY YOURS" CHOCOLATE CHIP BARS

¾ CRISCO® Stick or ¾ cup CRISCO® All-Vegetable Shortening
2 eggs
½ cup granulated sugar
¼ cup firmly packed brown sugar
1½ teaspoons vanilla
1 teaspoon almond extract
2 cups all-purpose flour
1 teaspoon baking soda
½ teaspoon ground cinnamon
1 can (21 ounces) cherry pie filling
1½ cups milk chocolate big chips
Powdered sugar

1. Preheat oven to 350°F. Grease 15½×10½×1-inch jelly-roll pan.

2. Combine shortening, eggs, granulated sugar, brown sugar, vanilla and almond extract in large bowl. Beat at medium speed of electric mixer until well blended.

3. Combine flour, baking soda and cinnamon in medium bowl. Mix into creamed mixture at low speed until just blended. Stir in pie filling and chocolate chips. Spread in pan.

4. Bake 25 minutes or until lightly browned and top springs back when lightly pressed. Cool completely in pan on wire rack. Sprinkle with powdered sugar. Cut into 2½×2-inch bars.

Makes 30 bars

California Apricot Power Bars

LAYERED CHOCOLATE CHEESE BARS

¼ cup (½ stick) margarine or butter
1½ cups graham cracker crumbs
¾ cup sugar
1 package (4 ounces) BAKER'S®
    GERMAN'S® Sweet Chocolate, melted
1 package (8 ounces) PHILADELPHIA
    BRAND® Cream Cheese, softened
1 egg
1 cup BAKER'S® ANGEL FLAKE® Coconut
1 cup chopped nuts

HEAT oven to 350°F.

MELT margarine in oven in 13×9-inch pan. Add graham cracker crumbs and ¼ cup of the sugar; mix well. Press into pan. Bake for 10 minutes.

COMBINE melted chocolate, the remaining ½ cup sugar, the cream cheese and egg. Spread over crust. Sprinkle with coconut and nuts; press lightly.

BAKE for 30 minutes. Cool; cut into bars.

Makes about 24 bars

Prep Time: 20 minutes
Baking Time: 40 minutes

BANANA SPLIT BARS

⅓ cup margarine or butter, softened
1 cup sugar
1 egg
1 banana, mashed
½ teaspoon vanilla
1¼ cups all-purpose flour
1 teaspoon CALUMET® Baking Powder
¼ teaspoon salt
⅓ cup chopped nuts
2 cups KRAFT® Miniature Marshmallows
1 cup BAKER'S® Semi-Sweet Real
    Chocolate Chips
⅓ cup maraschino cherries, drained and
    quartered

HEAT oven to 350°F.

BEAT margarine and sugar until light and fluffy. Add egg, banana and vanilla; mix well. Mix in flour, baking powder and salt. Stir in nuts. Pour into greased 13×9-inch pan.

BAKE for 20 minutes. Remove from oven. Sprinkle with marshmallows, chips and cherries. Bake 10 to 15 minutes longer or until toothpick inserted in center comes out clean. Cool in pan; cut into bars.

Makes about 24 bars

Prep Time: 20 minutes
Baking Time: 30 to 35 minutes

Top plate (clockwise from top): Layered Chocolate Cheese Bar, Banana Split Bar, Chocolate Peanut Butter Bar (page 36)

PEACHY OATMEAL BARS

CRUMB MIXTURE
- 1½ cups all-purpose flour
- 1 cup uncooked rolled oats
- ¾ cup margarine, melted
- ½ cup sugar
- 2 teaspoons almond extract
- ½ teaspoon baking soda
- ¼ teaspoon salt

FILLING
- ¾ cup peach or apricot preserves
- ⅓ cup flaked coconut

Preheat oven to 350°F.

For Crumb Mixture, combine all crumb mixture ingredients in large bowl of electric mixer. Beat at low speed, scraping bowl often, until mixture is crumbly, 1 to 2 minutes. *Reserve ¾ cup crumb mixture;* press remaining crumb mixture onto bottom of greased 9-inch square baking pan.

For Filling, spread preserves to within ½ inch of edge of crust; sprinkle with reserved crumb mixture and coconut. Bake for 20 to 25 minutes or until edges are lightly browned. Cool completely. Cut into bars. *Makes about 24 bars*

STREUSEL STRAWBERRY BARS

- 1 cup butter or margarine, softened
- 1 cup sugar
- 2 cups all-purpose flour
- 1 egg
- ¾ cup pecans, coarsely chopped
- 1 jar (10 ounces) strawberry or raspberry preserves

Preheat oven to 350°F. Combine butter and sugar in large mixing bowl. Beat at low speed, scraping bowl often, until well blended. Add flour and egg. Beat until mixture is crumbly, 2 to 3 minutes. Stir in pecans. Reserve 1 cup crumb mixture; press remaining crumb mixture onto bottom of greased 9-inch square baking pan. Spread preserves to within ½ inch of edge of crust. Crumble reserved crumb mixture over preserves. Bake for 40 to 50 minutes or until lightly browned. Cool completely. Cut into bars. *Makes about 24 bars*

Top to bottom: Peachy Oatmeal Bars, Streusel Strawberry Bars

LEMON NUT BARS

1⅓ cups all-purpose flour
½ cup firmly packed brown sugar
¼ cup granulated sugar
¾ cup butter
1 cup old-fashioned or quick oats,
**   uncooked**
½ cup chopped nuts
1 (8-ounce) package PHILADELPHIA
**   BRAND® Cream Cheese, softened**
1 egg
3 tablespoons lemon juice
1 tablespoon grated lemon peel

Preheat oven to 350°F. Stir together flour and sugars in medium bowl. Cut in butter until mixture resembles coarse crumbs. Stir in oats and nuts. Reserve 1 cup crumb mixture; press remaining crumb mixture onto bottom of greased 13×9-inch baking pan. Bake 15 minutes. Beat cream cheese, egg, juice and peel in small mixing bowl at medium speed with electric mixer until well blended. Pour over crust; sprinkle with reserved crumb mixture. Bake 25 minutes. Cool; cut into bars.   *Makes about 36 bars*

Prep Time: 30 minutes
Cook Time: 25 minutes

LUSCIOUS LEMON BARS

CRUST
½ cup butter or margarine, softened
½ cup granulated sugar
**   Grated peel of ½ SUNKIST® Lemon**
1¼ cups all-purpose flour

LEMON LAYER
4 eggs
1⅔ cups granulated sugar
3 tablespoons all-purpose flour
½ teaspoon baking powder
**   Grated peel of ½ SUNKIST® Lemon**
**   Juice of 2 SUNKIST® Lemons**
**   (6 tablespoons)**
1 teaspoon vanilla extract
**   Powdered sugar**

For Crust, in medium bowl, cream together butter, granulated sugar and lemon peel. Gradually stir in flour to form a soft crumbly dough. Press evenly into bottom of aluminum foil-lined 13×9×2-inch baking pan. Bake at 350° for 15 minutes.

For Lemon Layer, while crust is baking, in large bowl, whisk or beat eggs well. Stir together granulated sugar, flour and baking powder. Gradually whisk sugar mixture into eggs. Whisk in lemon peel, juice and vanilla. Pour over hot crust. Return to oven. Bake for 20 to 25 minutes or until top is lightly browned. Cool. Using foil on two sides, lift out cookie base. Gently loosen foil along all sides. With long wet knife, cut into bars or squares. Sprinkle tops with powdered sugar.
Makes about 3 dozen bars

Lemon Nut Bars

HEATH® BARS

- **1 cup butter, softened**
- **1 cup firmly packed brown sugar**
- **1 egg yolk**
- **1 teaspoon vanilla**
- **2 cups all-purpose flour**
- **18 to 19 Original HEATH® English Toffee Snack Size Bars, crushed, divided**
- **½ cup finely chopped pecans**

Preheat oven to 350°F. In large bowl, with electric mixer, beat butter well; blend in brown sugar, egg yolk and vanilla. By hand, mix in flour, ⅔ cup Heath® Bars and nuts. Press into ungreased 15½×10½-inch jelly-roll pan.

Bake 18 to 20 minutes or until browned. Remove from oven and immediately sprinkle remaining Heath® Bars over top. Cool slightly; cut into bars while warm. *Makes about 48 bars*

CHOCOLATE PEANUT BUTTER BARS

- **2 cups peanut butter**
- **1 cup sugar**
- **2 eggs**
- **1 package (8 ounces) BAKER'S® Semi-Sweet Chocolate**
- **1 cup chopped peanuts**

HEAT oven to 350°F.

BEAT peanut butter, sugar and eggs in large bowl until light and fluffy. Reserve 1 cup peanut butter mixture; set aside.

MELT four squares of the chocolate. Add to peanut butter mixture in bowl; mix well. Press into ungreased 13×9-inch pan. Top with reserved peanut butter mixture.

BAKE for 30 minutes or until edges are lightly browned. Melt the remaining 4 squares chocolate; spread evenly over entire surface. Sprinkle with peanuts. Cool in pan until chocolate is set. Cut into bars. *Makes about 24 bars*

Prep Time: 15 minutes
Baking Time: 30 minutes

Heath® Bars

Brownies

DECADENT BLONDE BROWNIES

½ cup butter or margarine, softened
¾ cup granulated sugar
¾ cup firmly packed light brown sugar
2 large eggs
2 teaspoons vanilla
1½ cups all-purpose flour
1 teaspoon baking powder
½ teaspoon salt
1 package (10 ounces) semisweet chocolate chunks
1 jar (3½ ounces) macadamia nuts, coarsely chopped

Preheat oven to 350°F. Beat butter, granulated sugar and brown sugar in large bowl with electric mixer at medium speed until light and fluffy. Beat in eggs and vanilla. Add combined flour, baking powder and salt. Stir until well blended. Stir in chocolate chunks and macadamia nuts. Spread evenly into greased 13×9-inch baking pan. Bake 25 to 30 minutes or until golden brown. Remove pan to wire rack; cool completely. Cut into 3¼×1½-inch bars.   *Makes about 2 dozen brownies*

RASPBERRY FUDGE BROWNIES

- ½ cup butter or margarine
- 3 squares (1 ounce each) bittersweet chocolate*
- 2 eggs
- 1 cup sugar
- 1 teaspoon vanilla
- ¾ cup all-purpose flour
- ¼ teaspoon baking powder
  Dash salt
- ½ cup sliced or slivered almonds
- ½ cup raspberry preserves
- 1 cup (6 ounces) milk chocolate chips

*Bittersweet chocolate is available in specialty food stores. One square unsweetened chocolate plus 2 squares semisweet chocolate may be substituted.

Preheat oven to 350°F. Butter and flour 8-inch square baking pan. Melt butter and bittersweet chocolate in small, heavy saucepan over low heat. Remove from heat; cool. Beat eggs, sugar and vanilla in large bowl until light. Beat in chocolate mixture. Stir in flour, baking powder and salt until just blended. Spread ¾ of batter in prepared pan; sprinkle almonds over top. Bake 10 minutes. Remove from oven; spread preserves over almonds. Carefully spoon remaining batter over preserves, smoothing top. Bake 25 to 30 minutes or just until top feels firm. Remove from oven; sprinkle chocolate chips over top. Let stand a few minutes, then spread evenly over brownies. Cool completely. When chocolate is set, cut into squares.

Makes 16 brownies

WHITE CHOCOLATE CHUNK BROWNIES

- 4 squares (1 ounce each) unsweetened chocolate, coarsely chopped
- ½ cup butter or margarine
- 2 large eggs
- 1¼ cups granulated sugar
- 1 teaspoon vanilla
- ½ cup all-purpose flour
- ½ teaspoon salt
- 1 white baking bar (6 ounces), cut into ¼-inch pieces
- ½ cup coarsely chopped walnuts (optional)
  Powdered sugar for garnish

Preheat oven to 350°F. Melt unsweetened chocolate and butter in small, heavy saucepan over low heat, stirring constantly; set aside. Beat eggs in large bowl; gradually add granulated sugar, beating at medium speed about 4 minutes until very thick and lemon colored. Beat in chocolate mixture and vanilla. Beat in flour and salt just until blended. Stir in baking bar pieces and walnuts. Spread evenly into greased 8-inch square baking pan. Bake 30 minutes or until edges begin to pull away from sides of pan and center is set. Remove pan to wire rack; cool completely. Cut into 2-inch squares. Sprinkle with powdered sugar, if desired.

Makes about 16 brownies

Raspberry Fudge Brownies

TOFFEE BROWNIE BARS

CRUST
- ¾ cup butter or margarine, softened
- ¾ cup firmly packed brown sugar
- 1 egg yolk
- ¾ teaspoon vanilla extract
- 1½ cups all-purpose flour

FILLING
- 1 package (19.8 ounces) DUNCAN HINES® Fudge Brownie Mix
- 1 egg
- ⅓ cup water
- ⅓ cup CRISCO® Oil

TOPPING
- 1 package (12 ounces) milk chocolate chips, melted
- ¾ cup finely chopped pecans

1. Preheat oven to 350°F. Grease 15½×10½×1-inch jelly-roll pan.

2. For Crust, combine butter, brown sugar, egg yolk and vanilla extract in large bowl. Stir in flour. Spread in pan. Bake 15 minutes or until golden.

3. For Filling, combine brownie mix, egg, water and oil in large bowl. Stir with spoon until well blended, about 50 strokes. Spread over hot crust. Bake 15 minutes or until surface appears set. Cool 30 minutes.

4. For Topping, spread melted chocolate on top of brownie layer; garnish with pecans. Cool completely in pan on wire rack. Cut into bars.

Makes about 48 brownies

EXTRA MOIST & CHUNKY BROWNIES

- 1 (8-ounce) package cream cheese, softened
- 1 cup sugar
- 1 egg
- 1 teaspoon vanilla extract
- ¾ cup all-purpose flour
- 1 (4-serving size) package ROYAL® Chocolate or Dark 'n' Sweet Chocolate Pudding & Pie Filling
- 4 (1-ounce) semisweet chocolate squares, chopped

MICROWAVE DIRECTIONS: In large bowl, with electric mixer at high speed, beat cream cheese, sugar, egg and vanilla until smooth; blend in flour and pudding mix. Spread batter in greased 8×8×2-inch microwavable dish; sprinkle with chocolate. Microwave on HIGH (100% power) for 8 to 10 minutes or until toothpick inserted in center comes out clean, rotating dish ½ turn every 2 minutes. Cool completely in pan. Cut into squares.

Makes 16 brownies

Toffee Brownie Bars

CARAMEL–LAYERED BROWNIES

    4 squares BAKER'S® Unsweetened Chocolate
    ¾ cup (1½ sticks) margarine or butter
    2 cups sugar
    3 eggs
    1 teaspoon vanilla
    1 cup all-purpose flour
    1 cup BAKER'S® Semi-Sweet Real Chocolate Chips
    1½ cups chopped nuts
    1 package (14 ounces) caramels
    ⅓ cup evaporated milk

HEAT oven to 350°F.

MICROWAVE chocolate and margarine in large microwavable bowl on HIGH 2 minutes or until margarine is melted. **Stir until chocolate is completely melted.**

STIR sugar into melted chocolate mixture. Mix in eggs and vanilla until well blended. Stir in flour. Remove 1 cup of batter; set aside. Spread remaining batter in greased 13×9-inch pan. Sprinkle with chips and 1 cup of the nuts.

MICROWAVE caramels and milk in same bowl on HIGH 4 minutes, stirring after 2 minutes. Stir until caramels are completely melted and smooth. Spoon over chips and nuts, spreading to edges of pan. Gently spread reserved batter over caramel mixture. Sprinkle with the remaining ½ cup nuts.

BAKE for 40 minutes or until toothpick inserted into center comes out with fudgy crumbs. **Do not overbake.** Cool in pan; cut into squares.

Makes about 24 brownies

BLONDE BRICKLE BROWNIES

    1⅓ cups all-purpose flour
    ½ teaspoon baking powder
    ¼ teaspoon salt
    2 eggs
    ½ cup granulated sugar
    ½ cup firmly packed brown sugar
    ⅓ cup butter or margarine, melted
    1 teaspoon vanilla
    ¼ teaspoon almond extract
    1 package (6 ounces) BITS 'O BRICKLE®, divided
    ½ cup chopped pecans (optional)

Preheat oven to 350°F. Grease 8-inch square baking pan. Mix flour with baking powder and salt; set aside. In large bowl, beat eggs well. Gradually beat in granulated sugar and brown sugar until thick and creamy. Add butter, vanilla and almond extract; mix well. Gently stir in flour mixture until moistened. Fold in ⅔ cup Bits 'O Brickle® and nuts. Pour into prepared pan.

Bake 30 minutes. Remove from oven; immediately sprinkle remaining Bits 'O Brickle® over top. Cool completely in pan on wire rack. Cut into squares.

Makes about 16 brownies

Blonde Brickle Brownies

Delights

CHOCOLATE CHIP LOLLIPOPS

**1 package DUNCAN HINES® Chocolate Chip
   Cookie Mix**
1 egg
⅓ cup CRISCO® Oil
2 tablespoons water
   Flat ice cream sticks
   Assorted decors

1. Preheat oven to 375°F.

2. Combine cookie mix, egg, oil and water in large bowl. Stir until thoroughly blended. Shape dough into 32 (1-inch) balls. Place balls 3 inches apart on ungreased cookie sheets. Push ice cream stick into center of each ball. Flatten dough ball with hand to form round lollipop. Decorate by pressing decors onto dough. Bake at 375°F for 8 to 9 minutes or until light golden brown. Cool 1 minute on cookie sheets. Remove to wire racks. Cool completely. Store in airtight container.

Makes 2½ to 3 dozen cookies

PEANUT BUTTER BEARS

   1 cup **SKIPPY®** Creamy Peanut Butter
   1 cup **MAZOLA®** Margarine, softened
   1 cup firmly packed brown sugar
   ⅔ cup **KARO®** Light or Dark Corn Syrup
   2 eggs
   4 cups all-purpose flour, divided
   1 tablespoon baking powder
   1 teaspoon ground cinnamon (optional)
   ¼ teaspoon salt

In large bowl, with mixer at medium speed, beat peanut butter, margarine, brown sugar, corn syrup and eggs until smooth. Reduce speed; beat in 2 cups of the flour, the baking powder, cinnamon and salt. With spoon, stir in remaining 2 cups flour. Wrap dough in plastic wrap; refrigerate 2 hours.

Preheat oven to 325°F. Divide dough in half; set aside half. On floured surface, roll out half the dough to ⅛-inch thickness. Cut with floured bear cookie cutter. Repeat with remaining dough. Bake on ungreased cookie sheets 10 minutes or until lightly browned. Remove from cookie sheets; cool completely on wire rack. Decorate as desired.

Makes about 3 dozen bears

Prep Time: 35 minutes, plus chilling
Bake Time: 10 minutes, plus cooling

NOTE: Use scraps of dough to make bear faces. Make one small ball of dough for muzzle. Form 3 smaller balls of dough and press gently to create eyes and nose; bake as directed. If desired, use frosting to create paws, ears and bow ties.

MARSHMALLOW KRISPIE BARS

   1 package (19.8 ounces) **DUNCAN HINES®** Fudge Brownie Mix
   1 package (10½ ounces) miniature marshmallows
   1½ cups semi-sweet chocolate chips
   1 cup **JIF®** Creamy Peanut Butter
   1 tablespoon butter or margarine
   1½ cups crisp rice cereal

1. Preheat oven to 350°F. Grease bottom of 13×9×2-inch baking pan.

2. Prepare and bake brownies following package directions for original recipe. Remove from oven. Sprinkle marshmallows on hot brownies. Return to oven. Bake for 3 minutes longer.

3. Place chocolate chips, peanut butter and butter in medium saucepan. Cook on low heat, stirring constantly, until chips are melted. Add rice cereal; mix well. Spread mixture over marshmallow layer. Refrigerate until chilled. Cut into bars.

Makes 24 bars

Peanut Butter Bears

WATERMELON SLICES

 **1 package DUNCAN HINES® Golden Sugar
    Cookie Mix**
 1 egg
 ¼ cup CRISCO® Oil
 1½ tablespoons water
 12 drops red food coloring
 5 drops green food coloring
    Chocolate sprinkles

1. Combine cookie mix, egg, oil and water in large bowl. Stir until thoroughly blended; reserve ⅓ cup dough.

2. For red cookie dough, combine remaining dough with red food coloring. Stir until evenly tinted. On waxed paper, shape dough into 12-inch-long roll with one side flattened. Cover; refrigerate with flat side down until firm.

3. For green cookie dough, combine reserved ⅓ cup dough with green food coloring in small bowl. Stir until evenly tinted. Place between 2 layers of waxed paper. Roll dough into 12×4-inch rectangle. Refrigerate for 15 minutes.

4. Preheat oven to 375°F.

5. To assemble, remove green dough rectangle from refrigerator. Remove top layer of waxed paper. Trim edges along both 12-inch sides. Remove red dough log from refrigerator. Place red dough log, flattened side up, along center of green dough. Mold green dough up to edge of flattened side of red dough. Remove bottom layer of waxed paper. Trim excess green dough, if necessary.

6. Cut chilled roll with flat side down into ¼-inch-thick slices with sharp knife. Place 2 inches apart on ungreased cookie sheets. Sprinkle chocolate sprinkles on red dough for seeds. Bake at 375°F for 7 minutes or until set. Cool 1 minute on cookie sheets. Remove to wire racks. Cool completely. Store between layers of waxed paper in airtight container. *Makes 3 to 4 dozen cookies*

TIP: To make neat, clean slices, use unwaxed dental floss.

Watermelon Slices

PEANUT BUTTER PIZZA COOKIES

1 package DUNCAN HINES® Peanut Butter Cookie Mix
1 egg
¼ cup CRISCO® Oil
1 tablespoon water
Sugar
1 container (16 ounces) DUNCAN HINES® Creamy Homestyle Chocolate Frosting
Cashews
Candy-coated chocolate pieces
Gumdrops, halved
Flaked coconut
½ bar (2 ounces) white chocolate baking bar
1½ teaspoons CRISCO® All-Vegetable Shortening

1. Preheat oven to 375°F.

2. Combine cookie mix, peanut butter packet from Mix, egg, oil and water in large bowl. Stir until thoroughly blended. Shape into 12 (2-inch) balls (about 3 level tablespoons each). Place balls 3½ inches apart on ungreased cookie sheets. Flatten with bottom of large glass dipped in sugar to make 3-inch circles. Bake at 375°F for 9 to 11 minutes or until set. Cool 1 minute on cookie sheets. Remove to wire racks. Cool completely.

3. Frost cookies with Chocolate frosting. Decorate with cashews, candy pieces, gumdrops and coconut. Melt white chocolate and shortening in small saucepan on low heat, stirring constantly, until smooth. Drizzle over cookies.

Makes 12 large cookies

CRUMBLE BARS

½ cup butter or margarine
1 cup all-purpose flour
¾ cup quick-cooking oats, uncooked
⅓ cup firmly packed light brown sugar
½ teaspoon salt
½ teaspoon baking soda
½ teaspoon vanilla extract
4 MILKY WAY® Bars (2.15 ounces each), each cut into 8 slices

Preheat oven to 350°F. Lightly grease 8×8×2-inch baking pan; set aside.

Melt butter in large saucepan. Remove from heat; stir in flour, oats, sugar, salt, baking soda and vanilla. Blend until crumbly. Press ⅔ of mixture into prepared pan. Arrange MILKY WAY® Bar slices in pan to within ½ inch from edges. Finely crumble remaining mixture over the MILKY WAY® Bars. Bake 20 to 25 minutes or until edges are golden brown. Cool in pan on wire rack. Cut into bars or squares to serve.

Makes 12 to 16 bars

Peanut Butter Pizza Cookies

Holiday Treats

GOLDEN KOLACKY

1 cup butter, softened
4 ounces cream cheese, softened
1 teaspoon vanilla
1 cup all-purpose flour
¼ teaspoon salt
Fruit preserves

Combine butter and cream cheese in large bowl; beat until smooth and creamy. Blend in vanilla. Combine flour and salt; gradually add to butter mixture, blending until mixture forms into soft dough. Divide dough in half; wrap each half in plastic wrap. Refrigerate until firm.

Preheat oven to 375°F. Roll out dough, ½ at a time, on sugared surface to ⅛-inch thickness. Cut into 3-inch squares. Spoon 1 teaspoon preserves in center of each square. Bring up two opposite corners to center; pinch together tightly to seal. Fold sealed tip to one side; pinch to seal. Place 1 inch apart on ungreased cookie sheets. Bake for 10 to 15 minutes or until lightly browned. Remove to wire racks; cool completely.

Makes about 3 dozen cookies

LINZER SANDWICH COOKIES

1⅓ **cups all-purpose flour**
¼ **teaspoon baking powder**
¼ **teaspoon salt**
¾ **cup sugar**
½ **cup butter, softened**
1 **large egg**
1 **teaspoon vanilla**
Seedless raspberry jam

1. Combine flour, baking powder and salt in small bowl.

2. Beat sugar and butter in medium bowl with electric mixer at medium speed until light and fluffy. Beat in egg and vanilla. Gradually add flour mixture. Beat at low speed until dough forms.

3. Form dough into 2 discs; wrap in plastic wrap and refrigerate 2 hours or until firm.

4. Preheat oven to 375°F. Working with 1 disc at a time, unwrap dough and place on lightly floured surface. Roll out dough with lightly floured rolling pin.

5. Cut dough into desired shapes with floured cookie cutters. Cut out equal numbers of each shape. (If dough becomes soft, cover and refrigerate several minutes before continuing.)

6. Cut 1-inch centers out of half the cookies of each shape. Gently press dough trimmings together; reroll and cut out more cookies. Place cookies 1½ to 2 inches apart on *ungreased* cookie sheets.

7. Bake 7 to 9 minutes or until edges are lightly browned. Let cookies stand on cookie sheet 1 to 2 minutes. Remove cookies with spatula to wire racks; cool completely. To assemble cookies, spread 1 teaspoon jam on flat side of whole cookies, spreading almost to edges. Place cookies with holes, flat-side down, on jam. Store tightly covered at room temperature or freeze up to 3 months.

Makes about 2 dozen cookies

BANANA CRESCENTS

½ **cup DOLE® Chopped Almonds, toasted**
6 **tablespoons sugar, divided**
½ **cup margarine, cut into pieces**
1½ **cups plus 2 tablespoons all-purpose flour**
⅛ **teaspoon salt**
1 **extra-ripe, medium DOLE® Banana, peeled**
2 **to 3 ounces semisweet chocolate chips**

Pulverize almonds with 2 tablespoons sugar in food processor. Beat margarine, almond mixture, remaining 4 tablespoons sugar, flour and salt. Puree banana; add to batter and mix until well blended.

Using 1 tablespoon batter, roll into log then shape into crescent. Place on ungreased cookie sheet. Bake in 375°F oven 25 minutes or until golden. Cool on wire rack.

Melt chocolate in microwavable dish at 50% power 1½ to 2 minutes, stirring once. Dip ends of cookies in chocolate. Refrigerate until chocolate hardens.

Makes 2 dozen cookies

Banana Crescents

PEANUT BUTTER CUT-OUTS

½ cup **SKIPPY®** Creamy Peanut Butter
6 tablespoons **MAZOLA®** Margarine or
  butter, softened
½ cup firmly packed brown sugar
⅓ cup **KARO®** Light or Dark Corn Syrup
1 egg
2 cups all-purpose flour, divided
1½ teaspoons baking powder
1 teaspoon ground cinnamon (optional)
⅛ teaspoon salt

In large bowl, with mixer at medium speed, beat peanut butter, margarine, brown sugar, corn syrup and egg until smooth. Reduce speed; beat in 1 cup flour, baking powder, cinnamon and salt. With spoon, stir in remaining 1 cup flour.

Divide dough in half. Between two sheets of waxed paper on large cookie sheets, roll each half of dough to ¼-inch thickness. Refrigerate until firm, about 1 hour.

Preheat oven to 350°F. Remove top piece of waxed paper. With floured cookie cutters, cut dough into shapes. Place on ungreased cookie sheets. Bake 10 minutes or until lightly browned. *Do not overbake.* Let stand on cookie sheets 2 minutes. Remove from cookie sheets; cool completely on wire racks. Reroll dough trimmings and cut. Decorate as desired.   *Makes about 5 dozen cookies*

NOTE: Use scraps of dough to create details on cookies.

BAVARIAN COOKIE WREATHS

3½ cups unsifted all-purpose flour
1 cup sugar, divided
3 teaspoons grated orange peel, divided
¼ teaspoon salt
1⅓ cups butter or margarine
¼ cup Florida orange juice
⅓ cup finely chopped blanched almonds
1 egg white beaten with 1 teaspoon water
Prepared frosting (optional)

Preheat oven to 400°F. In large bowl, mix flour, ¾ cup sugar, 2 teaspoons orange peel and salt. Using pastry blender, cut in butter and orange juice until mixture holds together. Knead few times and press into a ball.

Shape dough into ¾-inch balls; lightly roll each ball on floured board into a 6-inch-long strip. Using two strips, twist together to make a rope. Pinch ends of rope together to make a wreath; place on lightly greased baking sheet.

In shallow dish, mix almonds, remaining ¼ cup sugar and 1 teaspoon orange peel. Brush top of each wreath with egg white mixture and sprinkle with sugar-almond mixture.

Bake 8 to 10 minutes or until lightly browned. Remove to wire racks; cool completely. Frost, if desired.   *Makes 5 dozen cookies*

Favorite recipe from **Florida Department of Citrus**

Peanut Butter Cut-Outs

PECAN DATE BARS

CRUST
⅓ cup butter or margarine
1 package DUNCAN HINES® Moist Deluxe
   White Cake Mix
1 egg

TOPPING
1 (8-ounce) package chopped dates
1¼ cups chopped pecans
1 cup water
½ teaspoon vanilla extract
   Powdered sugar

1. Preheat oven to 350°F. Grease and flour 13×9-inch pan.

2. For Crust, cut butter into cake mix with a pastry blender or 2 knives until mixture is crumbly. Add egg; stir well (mixture will be crumbly). Press mixture into bottom of prepared pan.

3. For Topping, combine dates, pecans and water in medium saucepan. Bring to a boil. Reduce heat and simmer until mixture thickens, stirring constantly. Remove from heat. Stir in vanilla extract. Spread date mixture evenly over crust. Bake 25 to 30 minutes. Cool completely. Dust with powdered sugar.   *Makes about 32 bars*

BLACK RUSSIAN BROWNIES

4 squares (1 ounce each) unsweetened
   chocolate
1 cup butter
¾ teaspoon black pepper
4 eggs, lightly beaten
1½ cups sugar
1½ teaspoons vanilla
⅓ cup KAHLÚA®
2 tablespoons vodka
1⅓ cups all-purpose flour
½ teaspoon salt
¼ teaspoon baking powder
1 cup chopped walnuts or toasted sliced
   almonds
   Powdered sugar (optional)

Line bottom of 13×9-inch baking pan with waxed paper. Melt chocolate and butter with pepper in small saucepan over low heat. Remove from heat.

Combine eggs, sugar and vanilla in large bowl; beat well. Stir in cooled chocolate mixture, Kahlúa and vodka. Combine flour, salt and baking powder; add to chocolate mixture and stir until blended. Add walnuts. Spread in prepared pan.

Bake in 350°F oven just until toothpick inserted into center comes out clean, about 25 minutes. *Do not overbake.* Cool in pan on wire rack. Cut into bars. Sprinkle with powdered sugar, if desired.
          Makes about 30 brownies

Pecan Date Bars

Acknowlegments

The publisher would like to thank the companies and organizations listed below for the use of their recipes and photos in this publication.

Best Foods, a Division of CPC International Inc.

California Apricot Advisory Board

Dole Food Company, Inc.

Florida Department of Citrus

Kahlúa Liqueur

Kraft Foods, Inc.

Leaf®, Inc.

M&M/MARS

Nabisco, Inc.

Nestlé Food Company

The Procter & Gamble Company

Ralston Foods, Inc.

Sunkist Growers

Index

~ METRIC CONVERSION CHART ~

VOLUME MEASUREMENTS (dry)

$\frac{1}{8}$ teaspoon = 0.5 mL
$\frac{1}{4}$ teaspoon = 1 mL
$\frac{1}{2}$ teaspoon = 2 mL
$\frac{3}{4}$ teaspoon = 4 mL
1 teaspoon = 5 mL
1 tablespoon = 15 mL
2 tablespoons = 30 mL
$\frac{1}{4}$ cup = 60 mL
$\frac{1}{3}$ cup = 75 mL
$\frac{1}{2}$ cup = 125 mL
$\frac{2}{3}$ cup = 150 mL
$\frac{3}{4}$ cup = 175 mL
1 cup = 250 mL
2 cups = 1 pint = 500 mL
3 cups = 750 mL
4 cups = 1 quart = 1 L

VOLUME MEASUREMENTS (fluid)

1 fluid ounce (2 tablespoons) = 30 mL
4 fluid ounces ($\frac{1}{2}$ cup) = 125 mL
8 fluid ounces (1 cup) = 250 mL
12 fluid ounces ($1\frac{1}{2}$ cups) = 375 mL
16 fluid ounces (2 cups) = 500 mL

WEIGHTS (mass)

$\frac{1}{2}$ ounce = 15 g
1 ounce = 30 g
3 ounces = 90 g
4 ounces = 120 g
8 ounces = 225 g
10 ounces = 285 g
12 ounces = 360 g
16 ounces = 1 pound = 450 g

DIMENSIONS

$\frac{1}{16}$ inch = 2 mm
$\frac{1}{8}$ inch = 3 mm
$\frac{1}{4}$ inch = 6 mm
$\frac{1}{2}$ inch = 1.5 cm
$\frac{3}{4}$ inch = 2 cm
1 inch = 2.5 cm

OVEN TEMPERATURES

250°F = 120°C
275°F = 140°C
300°F = 150°C
325°F = 160°C
350°F = 180°C
375°F = 190°C
400°F = 200°C
425°F = 220°C
450°F = 230°C

BAKING PAN SIZES

Utensil	Size in Inches/Quarts	Metric Volume	Size in Centimeters
Baking or Cake Pan (square or rectangular)	8×8×2	2 L	20×20×5
	9×9×2	2.5 L	22×22×5
	12×8×2	3 L	30×20×5
	13×9×2	3.5 L	33×23×5
Loaf Pan	8×4×3	1.5 L	20×10×7
	9×5×3	2 L	23×13×7
Round Layer Cake Pan	8×1½	1.2 L	20×4
	9×1½	1.5 L	23×4
Pie Plate	8×1¼	750 mL	20×3
	9×1¼	1 L	23×3
Baking Dish or Casserole	1 quart	1 L	—
	1½ quart	1.5 L	—
	2 quart	2 L	—